A Note from
Mary Pope Osborne About the

MAGIC TREE HOUSE®
FACT TRACKERS

When I write Magic Tree House® adventures, I love including facts about the times and places Jack and Annie visit. But when readers finish these adventures, I want them to learn even more. So that's why my husband, Will, and my sister, Natalie Pope Boyce, and I write a series of nonfiction books that are companions to the fiction titles in the Magic Tree House® series. We call these books Fact Trackers because we love to track the facts! Whether we're researching dinosaurs, pyramids, Pilgrims, sea monsters, or cobras, we're always amazed at how wondrous and surprising the real world is. We want you to experience the same wonder we do—so get out your pencils and notebooks and hit the trail with us. You can be a Magic Tree House® Fact Tracker, too!

Mary Pope Osborne

Here's what kids, parents, and teachers have to say about the Magic Tree House® Fact Trackers:

"They are so good. I can't wait for the next one. All I can say for now is prepare to be amazed!" —Alexander N.

"I have read every Magic Tree House book there is. The [Fact Trackers] are a thrilling way to get more information about the special events in the story." —John R.

"These are fascinating nonfiction books that enhance the magical time-traveling adventures of Jack and Annie. I love these books, especially *American Revolution*. I was learning so much, and I didn't even know it!" —Tori Beth S.

"[They] are an excellent 'behind-the-scenes' look at what the [Magic Tree House fiction] has started in your imagination! You can't buy one without the other; they are such a complement to one another." —Erika N., mom

"Magic Tree House [Fact Trackers] took my children on a journey from Frog Creek, Pennsylvania, to so many significant historical events! The detailed manuals are a remarkable addition to the classic fiction Magic Tree House books we adore!" —Jenny S., mom

"[They] are very useful tools in my classroom, as they allow for students to be part of the planning process. Together, we find facts in the [Fact Trackers] to extend the learning introduced in the fictional companions. Researching and planning classroom activities, such as our class Olympics based on facts found in *Ancient Greece and the Olympics*, help create a genuine love for learning!" —Paula H., teacher

**Magic Tree House®
Fact Tracker**

DOGSLEDDING AND EXTREME SPORTS

A nonfiction companion to
Magic Tree House® #54:
Balto of the Blue Dawn

by Mary Pope Osborne
and Natalie Pope Boyce

illustrated by Carlo Molinari

A STEPPING STONE BOOK™
Random House 🏠 New York

The Magic Tree House Fact Tracker series was formerly known as the
Magic Tree House Research Guide series.

Visit us on the Web!
SteppingStonesBooks.com
MagicTreeHouse.com

Educators and librarians, for a variety of teaching tools, visit us at
RHTeachersLibrarians.com

Library of Congress Cataloging-in-Publication Data
Osborne, Mary Pope, author.
Dogsledding and extreme sports : a nonfiction companion to Magic tree house
#54, Balto of the blue dawn / by Mary Pope Osborne and Natalie Pope Boyce ;
illustrated by Carlo Molinari.
p. cm. — (Magic tree house fact tracker)
"A Stepping Stone Book."
Summary: "A nonfiction companion to Magic Tree House #54: Balto of the Blue
Dawn."— Provided by publisher.
Audience: Ages 6–9. Audience: K to grade 3.
ISBN 978-0-385-38644-9 (trade) — ISBN 978-0-385-38645-6 (lib. bdg.) —
ISBN 978-0-385-38646-3 (ebook)
1. Balto (Dog)—Juvenile literature. 2. Iditarod (Race)—Juvenile literature.
3. Dogsledding—Juvenile literature. 4. Endurance sports—Juvenile literature.
I. Boyce, Natalie Pope, author. II. Molinari, Carlo, illustrator. III. Osborne, Mary
Pope. Balto of the blue dawn. IV. Title. V. Series: Magic tree house fact tracker.
SF440.15.O83 2016 798.8'3—dc23 2015013852

Printed in the United States of America
10 9 8 7 6 5 4 3 2 1

This book has been officially leveled by using the F&P Text Level Gradient™
Leveling System.

For William P. Pope with love

Sled Dog Consultant:
DR. JERRY VANEK, sled dog veterinarian and musher

Extreme Sports Consultant:
THOMAS LIBARDI, director of fitness and facilities, Lenox Fit Inc.,
Lenox, Massachusetts

Education Consultant:
HEIDI JOHNSON, language acquisition and science education specialist,
Bisbee, Arizona

Special thanks to Mallory Loehr, Paula Sadler, Jenna Lettice, Heather Palisi,
Carlo Molinari, and as always, gratitude to our editor, Diane Landolf

DOGSLEDDING
AND EXTREME SPORTS

Contents

Dear Readers,

In <u>Balto of the Blue Dawn</u>, our adventures took us to the beautiful state of Alaska. While we were there, we helped Balto, a famous sled dog, deliver medicine to a town during a terrible blizzard in 1925. We've read a lot about the history of sled dogs in Canada and Alaska. We found out that there is a great dogsledding race called the Iditarod. It is known as an "extreme sport" because the racers travel over 900 miles!

We wanted to learn all we could about sled dog racing and other extreme sports. What we discovered was amazing! There are people who jump over the Great Wall of China

on skateboards. There are people who climb huge rock walls using only their hands and feet. There are people who do flips in the air on skis! All these sports take people to their limits. We thought you might like to know more about them.

So put on your helmets and strap on your seat belts. Let's get ready for some fun with dogsledding and other extreme sports!

Jack
Annie

1

Sled Dog Racing

The first Saturday of March in Anchorage, Alaska, is always a great day. The Iditarod (eye-DIT-uh-rod) Trail Sled Dog Race, the most famous sled dog race in the world, begins right in the middle of town.

The night before, trucks dump heavy loads of snow on the streets so the sled dog teams can make their way out of Anchorage. Early Saturday morning, trailers full of dogs, sleds, and supplies begin to roll into town. Soon the air fills with the sounds of barking and the noisy crowds gathering on the sidewalks.

About an hour before the race, Iditarod workers arrive at the starting line. Sled drivers hook their dogs up to the sleds and try to keep them calm.

Mushers are the sled dog drivers.

Flags from every country and state that the racers call home flutter in the breeze. An announcer yells out the names of the *mushers* with their teams.

The starting clock is set, and the countdown begins. Five, four, three, two, one . . . and they're off!

As the crowds cheer, a team leaves every two minutes.

The mushers and their dogs are headed to Nome, Alaska, a town about 1,000 miles from Anchorage.

An Extreme Sport

The Iditarod is a sport of *endurance* and skill. Like other extreme sports, it pushes people to the limit.

Endurance is the power to get through hardship and pain that lasts for a long time.

The sled dogs and their mushers endure days of hard running. The weather can drop to fifty degrees below zero Fahrenheit. High winds and blizzards often leave the trail covered with snow and make it hard to see.

Mushers and their dogs sometimes get frostbite or become too tired to go on.

It takes between nine and fourteen

Sometimes trail markers can get knocked over and teams can get lost during a storm.

days for most teams to finish the race. For the mushers and their dogs, each day must seem like a lifetime.

Going to Extremes

Extreme sports like the Iditarod are for people who feel good about taking risks. You might ride your bike for an hour, but would you ride it all day for twenty days, as riders in the Tour de France race do?

The Tour de France course is more than 2,000 miles long.

You might also enjoy climbing around on big rocks, but how about climbing up a 3,000-foot rock formation using only your hands and feet, as free climbers do?

The distance between New York City and Jacksonville, Florida, is almost the same as the length of the Iditarod. Just imagine leaving New York City and driving a dogsled all the way to Florida!

There is almost never any snow in Florida, so this would be extra hard!

History of Extreme Sports

There have been extreme sporting events throughout history. Gladiators in Rome fought to the death against each other and even against wild animals.

The pankration was a harsh wrestling and boxing contest. If one wrestler died, the other was the winner!

Thousands of people watched as athletes in the first Olympics competed in brutal chariot races or extreme wrestling matches.

Modern extreme sports started with

The club members also tried skiing on grass by attaching blocks of ice to their skis.

students in Britain who were members of the Oxford University Dangerous Sports Club. In the late 1970s, some of them decided to bungee jump off a bridge that was 250 feet high.

When people bungee jump, they tie specially made long rubber cords to their

Members of the Dangerous Sports Club often did stunts like bungee jumping in fancy clothes and top hats.

ankles. Then they dive headfirst off a very high place. The cord yanks them back up before they can hit the ground.

The students jumped from tall cranes and out of hot-air balloons. They also spent some time in jail for jumping from places where it was against the law!

In 1965, kids from Mexico, the United States, and Japan got together in Anaheim, California, for the first-ever international skateboarding contest.

These boys were skateboarding in 1960.

As skateboards got better over the years, kids started inventing really amazing tricks.

One of the first was the ollie. Alan Gelfand, a skateboarder whose nickname was Ollie, invented the trick in 1978. He was fifteen.

To ollie, skateboarders push their rear foot down on the back of their board. This movement sends the skateboarders up into the air. The board almost looks as if it's attached to the feet. (But it's not!)

Around the same time that skateboards became popular, a man named Sherman Poppen made the first snowboard so his kids could surf the snow.

Sherman called it a Snurfer.

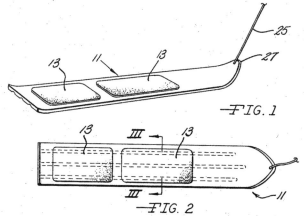

This illustration is from Sherman's 1966 patent application.

21

At first, some ski slopes banned snowboarding. Their owners thought it was too dangerous. But by 1998, snowboarding had become an Olympic sport.

In the summer of 1995, the sports television network ESPN began a sporting contest called the X Games. It is called the X Games because all the sports in it are extreme.

BMX bikes are special off-road bikes for racing and stunts.

Now there are summer and winter X Games every year. The games include sports like BMX biking, skateboarding, motocross, snowboarding, snowmobiling, and skiing.

Extreme Skills

Bungee jumping doesn't take much skill. But other sports such as snowboarding and rock climbing take a lot of practice.

Extreme sports are not usually team sports. Some of the athletes have coaches, but many work alone. They practice all the time to build up their skills.

This is also true of sled dogs and their mushers in the Iditarod. By the time the race rolls around, they have done more than 2,000 miles of practice racing together!

Arthur Joins the Team

In 2014, a team of extreme athletes from Sweden competed in the Adventure Racing World Championship. This endurance contest was very hard. The racers were supposed to run, trek, and kayak 430 miles through the steaming Amazon rain forests of Ecuador!

One day, a stray dog came up to the men as they were eating lunch. Someone threw him a meatball, and he gobbled it up. From then on, the dog stayed with them. The racers named him Arthur.

When the men had to kayak in a raging river, they feared Arthur would drown. They had no choice but to leave him on the riverbank. But Arthur jumped into the river and swam right alongside the boats!

Several days later, Arthur and the team crossed the finish line. The team captain adopted him. Now Arthur lives in Sweden. A favorite food there is Swedish meatballs. Arthur probably still loves them.

2

Sled Dogs

During the Ice Age, there was a land bridge across the cold Bering Sea from Alaska to a part of northern Russia called Siberia. About 12,000 years ago, people walked over it into Alaska and Canada. Their dogs trotted along with them.

About one-third of Alaska and Canada is in the Arctic. Much of the time, snow and ice cover the land. Long ago, there were no roads or cars. The native people counted on dogs and sleds to move themselves and their belongings around.

The dogs that came with them are related to most of the sled dogs today. Among them are Malamutes, Samoyeds, Siberian huskies, and Canadian and Greenland *Inuit* dogs called *quimmiq*.

The quimmiq almost disappeared, but people are working to keep this breed alive.

In the 1700s and 1800s, fur trappers and traders used sled dogs to carry furs and supplies.

In the late 1800s, explorers began trying to reach the North and South Poles. Many used sled dogs. They learned mushing skills from native Arctic people.

The Gold Rush

At the end of the nineteenth century, people found gold in Canada and Alaska. This news spread quickly, and the rush was on!

Thousands of people flooded into Canada and Alaska, hoping to strike it rich in the gold fields.

Mining camps sprang up and often turned into busy towns. Some of the most famous gold rush towns were Dawson

 Prospectors flock to look for gold in a part of Canada called the Klondike.

City in Canada and Nome, Fairbanks, and Iditarod in Alaska.

People needed a way to transport

furs, gold, mail, doctors, and many other things all over the country. They used dogs and sleds.

The Royal Canadian Mounted Police began using dogsleds in 1873.

Although Siberian huskies and Canadian Inuit dogs are good sled dogs, Malamutes can handle the heaviest loads. They can pull as much as 1,000 pounds!

When the gold rush was over, people kept using dogs and sleds. But as time passed, cars, snowmobiles, and airplanes took over.

What Is a Sled Dog Like?

Sled dogs need a lot of exercise. Because they're happiest running several hours a day, they're not good city dogs.

Sled dogs are creatures of the North. They feel best in cold weather. Their

31

bodies have special ways of surviving in the freezing temperatures.

<u>Eyes</u>: squint for protection from cold, wind, and glare.

Thick hair covers both the outer and inner <u>ears</u>.

<u>Two coats</u>: Undercoat shorter to hold in heat. Outer coat keeps snow and ice from building up.

<u>Big feet</u> with skin like thick leather covered in warm fur.

<u>Bushy tail</u>: Curls around the dog's nose when it's sleeping in snow.

Sleds

The early native people of the Canadian forests had flat sleds called toboggans for soft snow. The Inuit, who lived farther north, used a sled with two runners called a *komatik* (koh-MAH-tik). This worked well on ice or hard-packed snow.

Komatik

During the gold rush, basket sleds were popular on hard-packed trails. They had runners high enough to get through shallow snow and a place to store supplies.

Today's long-distance racing sleds combine toboggans and basket sleds for all kinds of snow. The runners look like skis, and there is a place on the sled bed

to store supplies or to carry sick dogs.

In the past, sleds were made of wood held together with rawhide. Now sleds are made from light materials like aluminum and plastic. They are lighter and stronger than the wooden ones. (Not good for chewing, either!)

The wood and rawhide sleds made yummy chews for the dogs!

Mushers

The word *musher* comes from French Canadian traders who called out to their dogs, *"Marche!"* It means "Move!"

Mushers stand on the back of the sled. They hold on to a handlebar and brace their feet on boards attached to the runners. They slow down by stepping on a mat that drags along the ground. To stop, they push on a metal brake with their feet.

35

Many mushers come from mushing families. Dallas Seavey won the Iditarod in 2012, 2014, and 2015. Dallas and his father, Mitch, who is also an Iditarod champion, have raced against each other in the last eleven Iditarods. And in 1973, Dallas's grandfather Dan ran in the very first Iditarod!

Sled dog racing is now the official sport

of Alaska. The people and the dogs that compete are all athletes. They live and train together. The bond between mushers and their dogs is strong. How else could they get through a race that's known as the Last Great Race on Earth?

Dallas Seavey poses with his lead dogs, Reef and Hero, after winning the 2015 Iditarod.

Reading the Signs

Since mushers spend so much time with their dogs, they know them well. One story is of a musher who knew that his lead dog never looked back at him. One day the dog kept turning its head to look back at the musher. It was so unusual that the musher stopped the sled. A cliff with a twenty-foot drop was right ahead!

Dogs have ways of showing their feelings. When their tails hang down instead of curling up, the dogs might be tired. If their back hair stands up or if they stare hard at another dog or curl their lips back, they're feeling threatened and might fight.

Mushers often say that their dogs are so close to them that each knows what the other is thinking.

3

The Iditarod

In 1925, Nome, Alaska, was in bad trouble. Some children were coming down with a serious disease called diphtheria (dif-THEER-ee-uh). A few had already died. People knew that this terrible lung disease could spread quickly. Everyone in town was at risk.

There was a serum to treat the disease. A train could bring it from Anchorage to Nenana, a town over 600 miles from Nome. The problem was that there wasn't a way

41

to get it to Nome. The only airplane had a frozen engine. In the winter, people could only get to Nome by dogsled on an ancient route that would later be used for a portion of the Iditarod Trail Sled Dog Race.

Mushers pitched in and organized twenty dog teams. The plan was to take the serum in relays. Each team would travel thirty to fifty miles before another took over.

A snowstorm was raging with high winds and blowing snow. At times, the temperature fell to sixty-four degrees below zero Fahrenheit.

Gunnar Kaasen and his team ran the last fifty-four miles of the trip. Gunnar said that sometimes the snow was so thick he couldn't see past his hands.

Balto, a black Siberian husky, was Gunnar's lead dog. People didn't think Balto

Gunnar Kaasen
and Balto

was much of a natural leader, but he turned
out to be a great one!

Balto stopped the team just as it was
about to plunge into an icy river. He stuck
to the trail when it was impossible to see.
After fifty-four dangerous miles, Balto led
his team into Nome.

It had taken twenty mushers and 150
dogs to get the lifesaving serum to Nome.
And they did it in just five and a half days!

The Iditarod

By the 1970s, dogsledding was dying out in Alaska. But in 1973, some people had an idea about how to keep the sport of mushing alive.

Today the race is held in memory of the heroic serum run mushers and their dogs.

They decided to hold a sled dog race that would go 1,000 miles from Anchorage to Nome. Part of the trail would cover the same route used to bring the serum to Nome.

They named the race Iditarod, an *Athabaskan* word that means "distant place."

Athabaskans are the native people from the forests in the middle of Alaska.

Today, the Iditarod takes place every March. About sixty to ninety mushers and teams of up to sixteen dogs sign up.

The trail goes over mountain ranges, frozen lakes, and flat plains; down the Yukon River; and through deep forests. On average, the dogs run ten to twelve

44

miles per hour, although they can reach twenty-five miles per hour for short periods.

To include more towns in the middle of Alaska, the race has two different routes. In even-numbered years, a section of the trail goes farther north. In odd-numbered years, part of it dips down to the south.

Iditarod is also the name of a gold rush ghost town and the nearby river.

Iditarod Map

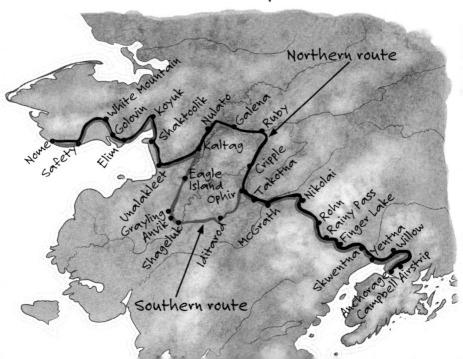

Northern route

White Mountain
Golovin
Koyuk
Shaktoolik
Nulato
Galena
Ruby
Nome
Safety
Elim
Kaltag
Cripple
Takotna
Nikolai
Unalakleet
Eagle Island
Ophir
Grayling
Anvik
Shageluk
Iditarod
McGrath
Rohn
Rainy Pass
Finger Lake
Yentna
Willow
Skwentna
Anchorage
Campbell Airstrip

Southern route

Training

Mushers can use many breeds of dogs for racing. Alaskan huskies are the number one choice for extreme mushing.

Mushers begin training dogs when they're puppies. At eight weeks, the puppies start wearing collars. A short time later, they get hooked up to harnesses and drag light objects around behind them.

Commands

The dogs have to learn these commands.

Jack and Annie's Sled Dog
Training School

All right! Okay! Hike! = Get going!
Gee = Turn right
Haw = Turn left
Easy = Slower
Whoa = Stop
Kissing sound (smack smack!)
or whistle = Faster

Getting Ready to Race

Training goes on all year round. The dogs on a team are usually between two and eight years old. The musher trains them to work well together. In most races, there are twelve to sixteen dogs. They work in pairs. The front two are the leaders.

Mushers can also signal turns by leaning right or left.

Mushers can spot good lead dogs while they're puppies. They are eager to lead. They are good at making decisions and staying on the trail. Lead dogs obey commands and control the direction and speed of the team.

Swing dogs run behind leaders. They, too, help turn the team. Next in line are the team dogs. They keep up the pace and pull the sled.

Wheel dogs are right in front of the

sled. They pull more of the weight, and some can sense how wide the turns should be.

In the winter, mushers often take practice runs of up to sixty miles a day. In the summer, the dogs normally rest because of the heat. Then in the fall, they practice on bare ground by pulling carts with wheels on them.

Wheeled cart

Diet

Alaskan huskies and other sled-racing dogs usually weigh around fifty pounds. Most mushers find that this is about the perfect weight for racing.

Trainers know that a good diet makes strong dogs. The dogs eat a mixture of kibble, fish, chicken, beef, and vitamins.

The dogs normally eat about a pound a day.

Mushers often chop up different kinds of raw meat and add hot water to make a stew for the sled dogs.

In the winter, chicken fat is added for extra pulling energy and to help the dogs stay warm.

When sled dogs aren't racing, they use about 1,800 calories a day. That's almost what an adult human needs. But when they're on the trail, they can burn up to 10,000 calories each day! Mushers usually stop about every four to six hours to feed the team. They also give the dogs tasty snacks every couple of hours.

When sled dogs are racing, they need more than a gallon of water for an all-day run. They get it from the food they eat and from drinking a warm broth that their mushers give them.

Getting Ready

Snowshoes

Ax

Extra-warm jacket

Vet's notes
on each dog

Along the Trail

Although mushers can stop anytime to rest
their dogs, rules say that each team must
take three big breaks. The first one lasts

Extra sets of strong cloth booties for each dog

Warm sleeping bag

Notebook for the race

Three-gallon pot for boiling water

Food for dogs and musher

for twenty-four hours. There are two eight-hour rest stops as well.

Mushers must also sign in at twenty-one checkpoints on the northern route and twenty-two on the southern. They pick up food and rest the dogs before racing away.

 Small planes drop bags of food and other supplies at the checkpoints.

There have been protests that too many dogs have died from exhaustion, sickness, or injuries during the Iditarod. Vets are on duty at every checkpoint to examine the dogs. A sick or hurt dog must be left at the checkpoint to be cared for.

Incredible Iditarod Stories

In 2014, Dallas Seavey broke every Iditarod record by nearly six hours. Dallas's total time was eight days, thirteen hours, and four minutes.

The slowest race was in 1974. The winner took twenty days and fifteen hours!

In 1985, Susan Butcher, a four-time Iditarod winner, was driving her team through a part of the trail known as Moose Alley. A moose charged them, killing two of her dogs and injuring many others. Susan had to drop out.

The most amazing finish was in 1978.

A few mushers carry guns in case of attacks by an angry moose.

Dick Mackey's team beat Rick Swenson's by one second. The tip of Dick's lead dog's nose crossed the finish line just barely ahead of Rick's.

In 1974, Mary Shields became the first woman to finish the race. Her lead dog was

named Cabbage. Mary said she named him that because he was "a silly-looking little puppy."

Libby Riddles was the first woman to win the Iditarod. In 1985, she and her team

fought their way through a horrible storm. The temperature reached fifty degrees below zero Fahrenheit.

Other mushers waited out the storm at a checkpoint. Libby took the chance to get ahead. She had to stop every hundred yards to wipe ice from her dogs' faces. At times, it snowed so hard that she couldn't

 Libby Riddles and her dogs Axle and Dugan make history at the 1985 finish line.

see the trail. But Libby blasted through to beat everyone!

The history of Alaska lives on in the sport of dog mushing. Most Alaskans don't need to compete in extreme races to keep this spirit alive. Many simply enjoy taking a short run with their dog teams on a cold winter's day.

The Widow's Lamp

Many years ago, it was a custom for a lighted lamp to hang outside inns where mushers stopped to rest. The lamp guided them in to a warm place, a hot meal, and much-needed sleep. It also let everyone know when someone was still on the trail. When the musher arrived, the lamp was put out.

At ten a.m. on the Sunday after the Iditarod begins, an official lights a lantern in Nome and hangs it on an arch at the finish line. When the last musher pulls in, the lamp is turned off. This means that every team has safely arrived and that the race is officially over.

4

Extreme Endurance

Many other extreme sports also call for endurance. Free climbers are a special kind of extreme athlete. They spend a lot of time climbing up steep rock walls without much equipment. The only help they have is safety ropes to keep from falling.

These athletes endure hours of slow and painful climbing. They inch themselves up the rock face by grasping tiny cracks in the wall with their fingers and feet. Then they use muscles in their arms and legs to pull themselves up.

The Dawn Wall

El Capitan is a gigantic rock formation in Yosemite National Park in California. One side of the rock, called the Dawn Wall, is

3,000 feet tall. Climbers had long thought it was impossible to free-climb this wall.

The wall has very few cracks for their hands and feet. Climbing the Dawn Wall even for a short time is very hard.

Rock climbers Tommy Caldwell and Kevin Jorgeson had tried and failed two different times. In January 2015, they tried again. They had trained for years to complete this climb.

Rock climbers take very good care of their hands. They coat them with climbing chalk to keep them from getting too sweaty and use special tape for protection.

Tommy and Kevin decided to climb in the winter to avoid the hot summer sun. They mostly climbed in the evening and at night to stay cool.

They wore headlamps to light their way.

As the men struggled up the wall, they had to hold on to rocks as sharp as razors. Their hands were raw and bleeding from cuts and scrapes.

In their downtime, they rested, ate, and slept in tents attached to the rock by ropes.

Sometimes they took several days off so their fingers could heal. They put lotion on them and filed their calluses down. They even sealed the wounds with superglue!

After nineteen days, the men arrived at the summit of El Capitan. Forty friends and family members had hiked up the back side of the rock and were waiting for them.

Everyone hugged and toasted their record-breaking climb. It was the first time anyone had successfully free-climbed the Dawn Wall.

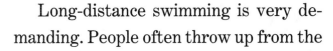
Diana Nyad

Extreme Swimmers

Endurance swimming is an extreme sport. Extreme swimmers go for miles in open water like the ocean or large lakes. Diana Nyad is one of the most famous endurance swimmers.

It is also called open-water or distance swimming.

Long-distance swimming is very demanding. People often throw up from the motion of the waves and from accidentally drinking salt water. Salt water also makes their throats and faces swell.

Jellyfish are another big problem. The stings from the box jellyfish, for example, are so toxic that people have died from them.

Some box jellyfish stings can kill a person in three to five minutes!

Swimmers also fight *hypothermia.* This condition sets in when the water temperature is lower than a swimmer's body temperature. It causes the blood flow to the body and brain to slow down. Hypothermia can lead to confusion and even death.

Diana and the Longest Swim

Despite all this, Diana has swum great distances. She became famous going 28 miles around the island of Manhattan. She also swam 102 miles from the Bahamas to Florida. Her biggest dream was to swim 110 miles from Cuba to Florida.

Manhattan is part of New York City.

Diana had tried it four times and failed. Strong winds, waves, currents, and jellyfish stings had stopped her. But when Diana was sixty-four years old, she decided to try again. On August 31, 2013, she began her greatest swim.

Shark-Free Swimming

The water between Cuba and Florida is full of sharks. Other swimmers who have tried this route did it inside a shark cage. Diana decided not to.

She wore a face mask and a bodysuit that prevented jellyfish stings. The face mask caused sores around her mouth, so she took it off.

Diana swam for almost fifty-four hours before she came ashore in Florida. That is well over two days of hard and dangerous swimming.

When Diana came out of the water, she was so tired she could barely walk. Her face was so swollen she could hardly speak.

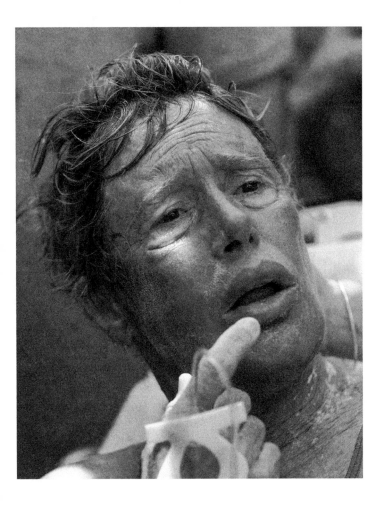

President Barack Obama sent her a tweet. It said *Never give up on your dreams*. Diana never did.

The Ironman

The Ironman triathlon is one of the most demanding extreme sports of all. A *triathlon* (try-ATH-lon) is three different sports in one event. The Ironman is the most extreme triathlon.

The sports are usually swimming, biking, and running. All of them take place on the same day. There is no time in between for the athletes to rest.

In order to become an Ironman, an athlete has to finish every sport within a certain amount of time. Women as well as men compete for this honor.

At seven a.m., the athletes begin a 2.4-mile swim. The swimming time limit is two hours and twenty minutes.

Then they leap out of the water, put on their biking gear, and race for 112 miles. The ride can't take longer than eight hours and ten minutes.

The last leg of the contest is a marathon run of 26.2 miles. It must be finished in six and a half hours. Athletes who stay within the time limits have the right to call themselves Ironmen.

Most athletes train about twenty-two hours a week.

75

The Iron War

The 1989 Ironman in Kona, Hawaii, has been called the Iron War or the greatest race ever. Along with thousands of others, two strong athletes, Dave Scott and Mark Allen, were competing to win.

Dave Scott

Mark Allen

Dave Scott was a six-time Ironman champion. Mark Allen was also an Ironman winner, but in the past, he'd lost five Ironman championships to Dave.

Both men had the fastest swimming times. In fact, they were exactly even. They also finished the bike race at the same time, ahead of everyone else.

The marathon was next. For miles, the men ran side by side. The crowds were

buzzing with excitement. It looked as if this Ironman was going to be a tie!

The athletes were only 1.7 miles from the finish line when they reached a small hill. Suddenly Mark pulled ahead of Dave. He raced to the finish line fifty-eight seconds ahead of Dave.

The men had finished three miles ahead of any other athlete. The whole Ironman had taken them just a little over eight hours.

Both men had broken world records. The hill where Dave fell behind Mark is now known as the Mark and Dave Hill.

Marathon

Legend has it that in ancient Greece, a messenger raced twenty-five miles from a battlefield in Marathon to the city of Athens. He was bringing the great news that Athens had beaten its enemies.

When the messenger arrived, he gasped out the word *"Niki!"* which means "victory." Then he collapsed and died from the hard run.

In 1896, the Olympics were in Greece. A long-distance race was one of the events. To honor Greek history, it was called a marathon. It was about twenty-five miles long.

In the 1908 London Olympics, Queen Alexandra wanted the race to begin at Windsor Castle so her children could watch. It was 26.2 miles from the castle to the Olympic stadium.

Since then, there have been marathons all over the world. And all of them are 26.2 miles long.

5

The X Games

In the 1990s, extreme sports were becoming more popular. In 1995, ESPN began a new event. It was to be like the Olympics for extreme sports. Since the sports in it were extreme, it was named the X Games.

The winter games are in Aspen, Colorado, and the summer games have been in Los Angeles, California, and Austin, Texas. They each last four days. As in the Olympics, athletes come from all over the world to compete for gold, silver, and bronze medals.

The Games

Sports in the Winter X are extreme skiing, snowboarding, and snowmobiling. They are different from regular sports because the athletes perform amazing tricks. Judges give medals to people with the best tricks and the most skill.

melon grab

roast beef

Some of the most extreme moves are in the slopestyle games for skiers and snowboarders.

In a slopestyle contest, athletes race down a course while doing tricks like mid-air jumps and triple flips. They are judged on how high and how hard their tricks are.

fakie

melon plant

Summer X Games

The Summer X Games include motocross, BMX biking, and skateboarding.

 Motocross riders do front flips and double backflips!

The Big Air event for skateboarders and BMX riders is really wild. People whiz down a huge ramp the size of a nine-story building. Then they leap over a gap about sixty feet wide, land on a smaller ramp, go back up the ramp, leap twenty feet in the air, turn around, and head back down!

So now let's go meet some great X Games champions!

Tony Hawk—Skateboarder

Tony is probably the most famous skateboarder ever. Although he was very smart, Tony was a hyperactive kid, especially in school. When he was nine, he got his first skateboard. Everything changed after that. Skateboarding calmed him down a lot. In just a few years, Tony was winning contests all over the state.

When Tony was fourteen, he became a professional skateboarder. He made so much money that he bought his first house before he finished high school!

By the time he was twenty-five, Tony had been crowned the skateboarding world champion twelve years in a row. Tony's

nickname was the Birdman. Can you guess
why? (Clue: What's his last name?)

Chloe Kim—Snowboarder

Chloe Kim began competing in snowboard contests when she was six. When Chloe was eight, she moved to Switzerland to live with her aunt and train in the Swiss Alps.

Chloe's sport is the superpipe. The superpipe is a ramp made of snow with a flat bottom and walls of snow on either side that are twenty-two feet high.

Chloe was only thirteen when she won a silver medal for the superpipe at the 2014 X Games. The next year she got a gold! Chloe was the youngest winner ever.

Chloe does forward flips called McTwists. In another trick, she spins around several times high up in the air.

Shaun White—Skateboarder and Snowboarder

With his red hair and wild boarding skills, Shaun's nickname is the Flying Tomato. He began skateboarding and snowboarding to be like his older brother.

When Shaun was sixteen, he started winning snowboarding medals at the X Games. He also won gold, silver, and bronze medals for skateboarding in the Summer X Games.

Shaun has won twenty-three X Game medals in snowboarding and skateboarding and two Olympic gold medals for the half-pipe.

He's known for the double cork trick. He flips sideways two times right in a row.

Shaun says that when you're at the

top of a ninety-foot ramp, you can't decide you're not going down. You're going down no matter what!

Travis Pastrana— Motocross Racer

Travis got a one-speed Honda when he was only four. By the time he was fifteen, he'd won an X Games gold medal. Travis also graduated early from high school. He was only fifteen when he went to college.

Travis is the first person to land a double backflip in a motorcycle competition. But his most famous trick is a one-hand fender grab Superman Indian air.

During this trick, Travis scissor-kicks his legs in the air and reaches back with one hand to grab the bike's fender while keeping his other hand on the handlebars!

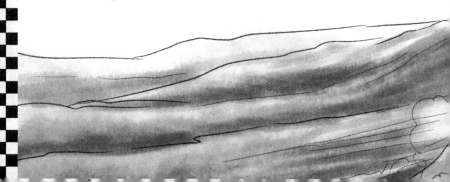

Jamie Anderson— Snowboarder

Jamie grew up in South Lake Tahoe, California. Her mom homeschooled Jamie and her seven brothers and sisters. She wanted them to love the outdoors.

While most kids were in school, Jamie's mother let her children ski, snowboard, and spend tons of time exploring nature.

When Jamie was thirteen, she competed in the Winter X Games. Two years later, she won a bronze medal in the slopestyle. Today she is a four-time X Games gold-medal winner.

Slopestyle became an Olympic event in the 2014 Winter Olympics. Jamie won the first Olympic gold medal.

Ryan Sheckler— Skateboarder

Ryan Sheckler was born in California in 1989. When he was eighteen months old, he found his father's old skateboard. He would push it around and try to ride it. By the time he was four, Ryan could ollie. At six, he was spending most of his free time practicing at skateboard parks or on the halfpipe in his backyard.

Ryan won his very first championship when he was seven. At the age of thirteen, he got a gold medal at the 2013 X Games. Ryan was the youngest X Games gold medal winner in history! Since then, Ryan has won many more medals. He's still thought of as one of the world's greatest skateboarders.

Ryan was so popular, he even had his own TV show called *The Life of Ryan*.

He says that when he was a kid skateboarding, he was just having fun. Even though he's now an adult, Ryan still loves the adrenaline rush of extreme skateboarding.

6

Why They Do It

Research shows that extreme athletes like the feeling they get from extreme sports. What else would make Yiannis Kouros, a Greek runner, run over 600 miles in six days with only two and a half hours of sleep? Or what would push Danny Way to jump over the Great Wall of China on his skateboard four times?

Certain athletes love extreme sports because of the way stress makes them feel.

The adrenal glands sit on top of the kidneys.

When humans get stressed, their adrenal glands give them extra energy by making their hearts beat faster. Blood rushes into their muscles and brains and gives them instant energy.

This burst of energy is called an *adrenaline* (uh-DREN-uh-lin) *rush*. People find that the rush makes them stronger and faster.

Extreme athletes say they feel most alive when this rush kicks in. At times when other people would be scared, extreme athletes feel great.

Another brain chemical that gives a sense of reward is called dopamine (DOPE-uh-meen).

Researchers have found that there are other brain chemicals at work, too. They make extreme athletes feel good whenever they take risks and push themselves. This feeling of well-being and happiness is the reward that extreme sports gives them.

Risks

Although not a lot of athletes in extreme sports die, many get hurt. Dr. Vani Sabesan, an expert on sports injuries, did a study of extreme athletes. She found that from 2000 through 2011, as many as four million extreme athletes were injured. Forty thousand of them suffered head or neck injuries.

Most of the neck and head injuries were from snowboarding and skateboarding.

Snowboarder Jackie Hernandez got a concussion when she fell in the 2014 Winter Olympics!

Even after terrrible injuries, many extreme athletes never give up. When Bethany Hamilton was thirteen, she was surfing in the Hawaiian Islands. A tiger shark attacked her and bit off her arm!

But Bethany didn't let that stop her. She is now a professional surfer who has won many competitions.

Bethany Hamilton

Because extreme athletes often set new goals for themselves, some sports are getting more extreme. The walls in halfpipes used to be eighteen feet tall. Now they are twenty-two. Some snowboarders are even using airbags to protect themselves!

Extreme athletes need to practice for years. You should never, ever try an extreme sport unless you have trained just as hard as they have with the help of great coaches!

The Need for Goals

Extreme athletes push themselves to do better every time they compete. Most of them say that they are really competing with themselves by setting goals and going for them. They feel most alive when they take risks and follow their dreams.

John Collins started the Ironman triathlon in 1978. He once said that you can quit and no one will care—but you will know for the rest of your life.

You don't have to be an extreme athlete to feel good about yourself. Everyone needs to move, and there is a sport out there for almost everyone, even if it's just hiking on a bright fall day.

You can also go to baseball fields, basketball courts, soccer fields, or skateboard parks. While most of us aren't made for extreme sports, all of us feel better when our bodies are in motion. And when that happens, you just might feel extremely happy!

Doing More Research

There's a lot more you can learn about dogsledding and extreme sports. The fun of research is seeing how many different sources you can explore.

Books

Most libraries and bookstores have books about dogsledding and extreme sports.

Here are some things to remember when you're using books for research:

1. You don't have to read the whole book. Check the table of contents and the index to find the topics you're interested in.

2. Write down the name of the book.

When you take notes, make sure you write down the name of the book in your notebook so you can find it again.

3. Never copy exactly from a book.

When you learn something new from a book, put it in your own words.

4. Make sure the book is <u>nonfiction</u>.

Some books tell make-believe stories about extreme sports. Make-believe stories are called *fiction*. They're fun to read, but not good for research.

Research books have facts and tell true stories. They are called *nonfiction*. A librarian or teacher can help you make sure the books you use for research are nonfiction.

Here are some good nonfiction books about dogsledding and extreme sports:

- *BMX Racers* (Kid Racers) by Ellen C. Labrecque

- *The Bravest Dog Ever: The True Story of Balto* by Natalie Standiford

- *Skateboarding: How It Works* (The Science of Sports, Sports Illustrated Kids) by Emily Sohn

- *Snow Dogs! Racers of the North* (DK Readers) by Ian Whitelaw

- *Snowboarding* (Kids' Guides to Extreme Sports) by Bob Woods

- *Ultimate Sports* (Extreme Readers) by Teresa Domnauer

Museums

Many museums can help you learn more about dogsledding and extreme sports.

When you go to a museum:

1. Be sure to take your notebook!
Write down anything that catches your interest. Draw pictures, too!

2. Ask questions.
There are almost always people at museums who can help you find what you're looking for.

3. Check the calendar.
Many museums have special events and activities just for kids!

Here are some museums with exhibits about dogsledding and extreme sports:

- Dog Mushing Museum (Fairbanks, Alaska)

- Early Years of Motocross Museum (Villa Park, California)

- Iditarod Trail Sled Dog Museum (Wasilla, Alaska)

- International Swimming Hall of Fame (Fort Lauderdale, Florida)

- Skateboarding Hall of Fame and Museum (Simi Valley, California)

- Utah Snowboard Museum (Salt Lake City)

- World Snowmobile Headquarters (Eagle River, Wisconsin)

The Internet

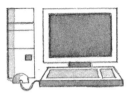

Many websites have lots of facts about dogsledding and extreme sports. Some also have games and activities that can help make learning about them even more fun.

Ask your teacher or your parents to help you find more websites like these:

- adventure.nationalgeographic.com /adventure/adventurers-of-the-year /2014/diana-nyad/
- discoverykids.com/activities /best-of-the-x-games/
- enchantedlearning.com/usa/states/alaska /iditarod/
- kidskonnect.com/fun/iditarod

- kidzworld.com/article
  /25052-shaun-white-bio

- news.nationalgeographic.com
  /2015/01/150113-climbing-yosemite
  -capitan-dawn-wall-caldwell-jorgeson

- timeforkids.com/news/mighty
  -mush-finish/151531

Good luck!

Bibliography

Buser, Martin. *Dog Man: Chronicles of an Iditarod Champion.* Durango, CO: Raven's Eye Press, 2015.

Fitzgerald, Matt. *Iron War: Dave Scott, Mark Allen & the Greatest Race Ever Run.* Boulder, CO: VeloPress, 2011.

Friel, Joe. *The Triathlete's Training Bible.* Boulder, CO: VeloPress, 1998.

Honnold, Alex, and David Roberts. *Alone on the Wall.* New York: W. W. Norton & Company, 2015.

Kotler, Steven. *The Rise of Superman: Decoding the Science of Ultimate Human Performance.* New York: Houghton Mifflin Harcourt, 2014.

Nyad, Diana. *Find a Way.* New York: Knopf, 2015.

Index

Photographs courtesy of:

Have you read the adventure that
matches up with this book?

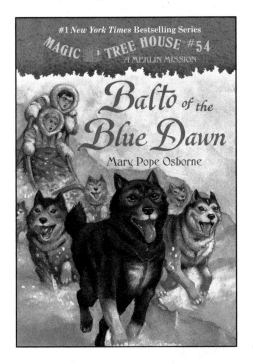

Don't miss Magic Tree House® #54
Balto of the Blue Dawn

Jack and Annie go back in time to 1925
Alaska, where a jet-black Siberian husky
named Balto needs their help!

Magic Tree House® Books

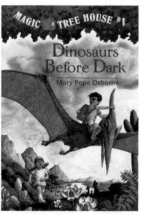

Magic Tree House® Fact Trackers

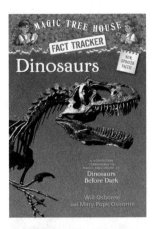

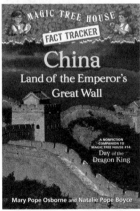

More Magic Tree House®